AGAINST ALL ODDS

Life is like a puzzle.
You put the pieces together to
get the whole picture.

SHEILA HODGES

authorHOUSE®

AuthorHouse™ LLC
1663 Liberty Drive
Bloomington, IN 47403
www.authorhouse.com
Phone: 1-800-839-8640

Scripture quotations marked NIV are taken from the Holy Bible, New
International Version®. NIV®. Copyright © 1973, 1978, 1984 by International
Bible Society. Used by permission of Zondervan. All rights reserved. [Biblica]

Published by AuthorHouse 04/10/2014

ISBN: 978-1-4918-6931-4 (sc)
ISBN: 978-1-4918-9914-4 (e)

Library of Congress Control Number: 2014905656

Any people depicted in stock imagery provided by Thinkstock are models,
and such images are being used for illustrative purposes only.
Certain stock imagery © Thinkstock.

This book is printed on acid-free paper.

DEDICATION

This book is dedicated to:

My husband: Mr. Hodges, dear mother, wonderful sons, grandchildren and great-grandchildren.

A special thanks to: First, oldest son who would not let me forget that I needed to write this book to inspire others that are facing similar obstacles. Last but not the least, my cousin and my granddaughter, I thank you both for your feedback, computer help, and editorial help.

AGAINST ALL ODDS

Not every teenager is willing to admit to failures and is willing to try to make amends. But, Wanda was such a person. As a result, of failures she was faced with educational struggles, teen pregnancy problems, and financial struggles. That is the opening line of Against All Odds. From the first line to the final paragraph, she created the obstacles by telling just enough to make readers ask questions that need good answers.

In the first chapters, she created obstacles by setting up an unstable childhood situation. Wanda grew up in a single parent home. Because her mother had to work all the time, she was unprotected and encountered abuse from her older siblings and other abuse at different times from her parents. They lived in a very, very poor environment, moved around a lot, and she went to different schools as a result.

Matthew 25:31 – 40.

The Sheep and the Goats

31 "When the Son of Man comes in his glory, and all the angels with him, he will sit on his glorious throne. 32 All the nations will be gathered before him, and he will separate the people one from another as a shepherd separates the sheep from the goats. 33 He will put the sheep on his right and the goats on his left.

34 "Then the King will say to those on his right, 'Come, you who are blessed by my Father; take your inheritance, the kingdom prepared for you since the creation of the world. 35 For I was hungry and you gave me something to eat, I was thirsty and you gave me something to drink, I was a stranger and you invited me in, 36 I needed clothes and you clothed me, I was sick and you looked after me, I was in prison and you came to visit me.'

37 "Then the righteous will answer him, 'Lord, when did we see you hungry and feed you, or thirsty and give you something to drink? 38 When did we see you a stranger and invite you in, or needing clothes and clothe you? 39 When did we see you sick or in prison and go to visit you?'

40 "The King will reply, 'Truly I tell you, whatever you did for one of the least of these brothers and sisters of mine, you did for me.' (Bible Gateway, 2011)

CHARACTERS

Main Character: Wanda Bethel-Canaan
Mother: Mary Bethel
Father: Jude Bethel
Brother: John Bethel
Brother: Luke Bethel
Brother: Solomon Bethel
Spouse: Judas Hope
Spouse: Timothy Canaan
Son: Joshua Canaan
Son: Isaiah Canaan
Son: Samuel Canaan
Son: Nehemiah Canaan
Son: David Canaan
Made Up Character: Jenny Sage
Made Up Character: Jackie Alabama

PURPOSE OF THIS BOOK

The purpose of this book is to share what happened in Wanda's life, in order to, encourage others who are considering settling for less. Also, to show that, it is not impossible to succeed. Life presents many obstacles, and our goals are sometimes difficult to obtain. However, as long as we have life there is hope. We must decide what we want, and go for it. Wanda decided early in life that she wanted more. Wanda knew faith in Jesus Christ, pursuing education and a career would help her to reach her goals.

CONTENTS

INTRODUCTION

Against All Odds is about Wanda's trials, and how she overcame them to reach her goals. She grew up in a single parent home which meant she was on her own because her mother worked all the time. Wanda lived in a very poor environment, and she moved around a lot. Furthermore, she went to a lot of different schools.

Wanda was the youngest of four children, and the only girl. Because her mother always worked, she was unprotected and she encountered abuse from her older siblings. This abuse and other abuse continued until she was about 13 years old when her mother made other arrangements for her to stay with her aunt, or her cousin. Sometimes, Wanda stayed with her mother's close friend.

Even though, Wanda got pregnant and married in her teen years, she decided to return to school, and complete her high school education. As a result, she encountered babysitting problems and spousal abuse. After several attempts to complete high school, and job training eventually she was successful.

During Wanda's adult years, her focus was employment and education. Both, opportunities are very important but they are not easy to obtain when you have other responsibilities and very little help. Sometimes, moving to another State might help brighten your future which is what she did.

Wanda accepted Jesus as Lord and Savior over her life; both, as a child and later as an adult. Wanda's Christian faith helped her to deal with her failures, calamities, tragedies, and Life as a whole.

1951 - 1964
WANDA'S CHILDHOOD

CHAPTER 1

On October 31, 1951, Wanda was born in Babylon, IL. She grew up in a single parent home, and lived in a very poor environment. She lived with her mother and three brothers as a child. She was the youngest of four children and was the only girl. Her mother's name was Mary, and her father's name was Jude. Wanda's father abused her mother, as a result her parents were divorced when she was very young. She didn't see her father often, but she loved him very much. He was a world war veteran. Wanda's mother was an Evangelist Preacher, she laid hands on the sick and prayed for them. She loved the Lord Jesus.

When Wanda was young her mother gave her vision, taught her to pray, and Psalms 91. Wanda's mother was very strict, she had to obey the house rules. When she was three years old, Wanda asked her mother what will she be when she grow up? Her mother said, "You will be a Teacher." (Proverbs 29:18 but blessed is the one who heeds wisdom's instruction. (Bible Hub, 2011) It's important to plant good seed in your children.

Until Wanda was about 8 years old, she would wake up, and get into bed with her mom. One night she got scared, and went to her mom's bed. She gave her Psalm 91 to read and Wanda returned to her own bed. Wanda stopped visiting her mom at night with fear. She started trusting God instead. Wanda's mother taught her to pray and to trust God! (Psalms 91:1-2). 1 Whoever dwells in the shelter of the Most High Will rest in the shadow of the Almighty. And 2 I will say of the Lord, "He is my refuge and my fortress, My God, in whom I trust." (Bible Hub, 2011)

Wanda's family were very, very, poor, they soften their beds with old clothes because they didn't have a mattress to sleep on. When Orange Castle Hamburgers were 12 cents. Wanda spent all day collecting soda bottles to cash them in, for a refund. Then, she bought cheeseburgers and an orange soda. Wanda loved Orange Castle Cheeseburgers. During that time food was cheaper, in fact, most food was less than a $1.00. Wanda's mother worked long hours, she was a housekeeper. Wanda cleaned the house, and ironed her brothers' shirts while her mom worked. Wanda's brothers worked paper routes. Her mother's employer gave her clothes, and she gave them to Wanda. Sometimes they were too big for Wanda, but she wore them anyway.

Wanda's family never stayed in one place too long. The first place they lived was on the west side of Babylon. Wanda was about three years old. They had a coal stove in the front room to keep warm during the winter. Her father told Solomon and Wanda not to run around the coal stove, it was red hot. However, her brother and Wanda was having so much fun they continue playing. So, when Wanda reached around the stove trying to catch him, her Right arm got stuck to the stove. Immediately, her dad took his belt off, snatched Wanda's arm off the stove, and beat her while holding her up by that arm. Wanda almost lost that arm, it was a third degree burn. Her mother was working at County Hospital as a nurse's assistant, but she couldn't afford healthcare. So, the hospital staff told her how to care for Wanda's arm. Her mother cared for her arm, but Wanda was in a lot of pain for a long time. John, said "One time Wanda had Scarlet Fever, she almost died, and that scared the family."

The second place they lived was the Projects on the west side of Babylon. Wanda was less than 7 years old. Her three brothers were mean to her most of the time. It was Christmas Day and her mother bought

2

her a brown Cowgirl outfit. They were playing Cowboys and Indians. Then, they hung Wanda and her dolls out of a 5th floor window. Her mother's friend came by to check on them because her mother had to work. She saw Wanda hanging by the neck while holding the rope to keep from strangling. The friend made Wanda's brothers pull her in. Then, the friend took Wanda to her house until her mother came home. This friend didn't have any children, she had very large eyes. Wanda's brothers didn't play with her, she looked mean but she wasn't. She fed Wanda at her house. After this, her mother never left her at home with them for a long time.

The third place they lived was on the north side of Babylon. It was a normal community. The shopping center was one block away. The pool hall was located on the corner of Wanda's street and across from the stores. That store was near a main street where the buses ran every 10 minutes. On the Fourth of July, they had block parties. Wanda lived in a 3 story apartment building. When she broke the house rules, her mother would tie her up, and beat her with an extension cord. After, she'd blister her mother would burst the whelps. Wanda's brothers would always get her into trouble by starting fights with her.

One day Luke spat in her face and he ran downstairs. Wanda couldn't catch him. So, she went to the window and dropped a soda bottle out of the window. It was good that she missed him because soda bottles didn't break easily back then. Wanda was angry when her mother hit her. So, she hit her back with a 2X4 (piece of wood) and her mother pushed Wanda out of the 3rd floor window. John caught Wanda by the hand while she was falling out of the window. Then, her mother was beating her hands, and John begged her to let him take the beating. She said, "No, and told him to tie Wanda up" and he did. She beat her with the extension cord and burst the whelps. This was Wanda's punishment when she broke the house rules. She was 13 years old at the time. After this, Wanda's mother started keeping her in when she broke rules. Even though they still moved a lot, this family stayed places longer, and they stayed on the north side of Babylon. Which meant Wanda didn't have to change schools as much as before.

Wanda's mother instilled family values in them. Those family values were Christianity, education, music, and holiday celebrations. Wanda went to different schools. However, there were two schools that made an impact on her life. The first school was a Catholic School located on the west side of Babylon. Wanda received her first Baptism and Confirmation at that Catholic Church. When she was nine years old, she told her Priest, "She wanted to be a Nun when she grows up." Pastor told her, "She would get married and have a lot of children." That Catholic School was her favorite school. Wanda had a friend there. She let her wear a gold watch, Wanda still wear gold watches today. The Nuns gave her mother shoes and uniforms for Wanda. Everything was so beautiful there.

The next school Wanda attended was a public elementary, she was in 8th grade. It was located on the south side of Babylon, she got into a great deal of fights. One day, Wanda's teacher pulled her ear, for talking in class. So, she hit her teacher in the stomach, she was expelled from that school. Wanda's mother enrolled her into a different elementary school. She graduated and received her elementary school diploma. Wanda's mother made her a white laced dress, and her research paper was on "How Paper is made from Wood?"

When Wanda was about 10 years old, she took vocal lessons on the south side of Babylon. Wanda's mother always took her to Church with her, and Wanda enjoyed singing during service. One day during a vocal lesson with Pastor, He told her, "You can sing, but I don't know where to put you because your voice is not developed yet. At home, she always sang and danced for pleasure. Now, Wanda is a Praise and Worship leader, and Soloist at Church.

Also, her mother always kept a piano in the front room. When Wanda was a young child, she used to play Mary Had a Little Lamb on the piano. Wanda plans to practice singing and playing gospel songs on the piano soon.

Wanda love special gifts, her family would give her special gifts during the holidays. Her aunt and her mother, knew that she wanted a sailor dress, baby doll shoes, and a walking doll. So, one Christmas Day, her aunt bought her two sailor dresses and black patent leather baby doll shoes. One was white with blue stripes and the other was navy blue with white and red stripes. Her mother bought her an African American walking doll which was very difficult to find during that time. The doll was taller than her, but Wanda took her everywhere. She was about 9 years old. Another special gift she received was during Easter, her mother and her brothers, gave Wanda a pink laced dress with red roses, and lite pink shoes. Her mother did her hair in a special way, Wanda was so happy, and she was at least 11 years old.

Holiday celebrations at home started with Wanda's mother. At first, her mother and Wanda cooked, she started helping her mother at a very young age, and then she helped every year to celebrate Thanksgiving and Christmas together as a family. It was a special time for them. They prepared special meals and shared time together. The family ate turkey and dressing, took family pictures, and exchanged gifts. Family members that could not come home during the holidays, they would call, or mail special cards. They also invited others to share the meals. Next, when Wanda's children were small she did all the cooking, but now her granddaughters help her with the holiday meals. Thanksgiving and Christmas was special, and still is a very special time to share quality time with the family.

What is a Traditional Thanksgiving?

A tradition is something that is passed down from generation to generation. Like a special dish, or special event that is done a certain way each year by the family. Thanksgiving Day is when the family come together, bless a special meal, thank God for what they have and don't have, eat the meal, and enjoy each other that special day.

Some family members that you have not seen for a while or they may live far away, will visit the family on that special day. Some families share the responsibility by everyone bringing a special dish to one destination. Whereas, other families nominate a person or persons to be responsible for this special meal, it will vary from generation to generation. However, it is done families should always honor their Traditional Day.

What is Family Support?

Family support is to encourage a family member, to take time to listen to your family members even though you think what they are saying is not important. Provide Godly counseling if needed and befriend your family member. Family support is when everyone else has given up on you, and still your family tells you that you can complete your task. It's being a team! Teamwork is to do your share and not to let one family member do everything by themselves. It's caring for each other, to be sensitive to one's feelings. Also, to acknowledge the good things about your family members.

In sum, family support is to celebrate success, to encourage a family member during failures, or trying times. It's something that everyone needs in life. Family support is love, empathy, compassion, and consideration for your family.

Wanda was abused by her siblings until age 9 years old. When she told her mother what was happening to her, she made other arrangements for her to stay with either her aunt, or her cousin. Sometimes, she stayed with one of her mother's close friends. She still experienced different abuse until she was 13 years old, but from her mother. When Wanda didn't follow the house rules, or when her brothers would get her into trouble which was most of the time. Wanda's mother always told her, "I don't care what those guys do, but you will be different." She always had to be with one of her brothers. Also had to be in the house BEFORE the street lights went out around 6 pm.

Everyone don't suffer from the same things. Some people struggle from babysitting problems, abusive marriage, lack of education, unemployment, loss of a loved one, and/or different kind of abuse. Some people will share their problems with you, and others will not tell you they have a problem. No matter if they have one, or many of these problems it can prevent them from reaching their goal if they don't deal with it.

Two examples of two victims that were molested and what they chose to do about it. The first, was a girl name Little Jenny. One day she got separated from her friends in a movie theater and a stranger approached her. He gave her treats to let him touch her inappropriately. She was under age 7 at the time. Jenny was molested until she was 8 or 9 years old by a family member. One day that family member took her under the stairs of their house and sold her for money. Also gave Jenny chocolate candy wrapped in gold paper to be quiet while they touched her in the wrong way. She told her mother, her mother sent Jenny to her aunt's house to stay while she worked. One day the aunt went to the store. Jenny was attacked, but that person did not succeed because Jenny was a good fighter and a good runner. Jenny told her aunt, she never had a problem again there. When Jenny was age 10 years old, her friend set her up for rape and she escape the rapist. Also, she decided to choose her friends more carefully. Three years later when Jenny was 13 years old, her boyfriend tried to rape her. She got away and never visited that boyfriend again.

The second example: A girl name Jackie who was being raped by her foster father. She never said a word to anyone. One day everyone knew because she became pregnant. The problem was she was only 10 years old. She made the news because it was a very unusual case.

That day when everyone found out, the police was all over the place! Everyone else just wanted to know what had happened in that home. They appeared to be regular people, Wanda would have never suspected anything like this. She used to visit and play with her often. Her foster mother gave Wanda food during the visit. She enjoyed her visit, everything looked normal to her. However, Wanda was very sad for her friend that day. A lot of bad things happened, some things changed for the better for her friend. Wanda was very young herself, so she could only speculate what more took place there that day.

Lesson to learn is, if someone tries to abuse you, or if they succeed in abusing you, TELL SOMEONE, who can and will help you. Or, else they will just keep abusing you. Until you do, or say something to stop them. Travel with a trustworthy friend, and don't accept gifts from strangers.

1965 -1974
TURNING FAILURES
INTO SUCCESS

CHAPTER 2

Public High School was fun and challenging. Wanda's freshman year in High school was exciting. She was a Cheer Leader which is every girl's dream, they wore green and white. Wanda loved it, she took cooking classes and orchestra band. They were fun classes!

In Wanda's sophomore year, she was learning to swim, it was a challenging experience. She was able to float and was not afraid of the water. The instructor told the class to jump in but Wanda hesitated. So, the instructor came up behind and pushed her in. Wanda went to the bottom of the pool and didn't come up. The water entered her nose and mouth. Wanda heard someone say "She is not coming up!" Wanda saw someone jump in. After, that she lost consciousness! Surely, the instructor got her out of the water. When she woke up the instructor was performing cardiopulmonary resuscitation (CPR). Wanda never went back to that class.

It was her junior year when she experienced her final challenge there, Wanda was on her way home from school when some girls jumped her because she was black, and Wanda fought them. Then their boyfriends jumped in but the onlookers stopped them. Next day, she was called to the office and expelled from High School for fighting. Then, Wanda's mother enrolled her in a Christian High School. At that school a girl warned her not to be the last one leaving because there had been reports of rape. Wanda tried to get out on time but she was new and it took her more time to pack up. That day Wanda was chased by a gang of boys to the bus stop. She almost missed the bus but the bus driver let her get on. So, Wanda was spared the abuse, she had only been there 3 weeks. Although, Wanda enjoyed her sewing class, she was learning how to make a two piece dark green leather outfit. Even though, she liked the school she never returned there.

During Wanda's high school years, she worked at Community Center as a teacher assistant (1965-1967). Wanda and her mother worked together some summers, her mother was an Art instructor. Wanda helped her with art projects and sometimes went on field trips. One day while she was on a field trip with the center, Wanda rode a horse that tried to jump a high fence with her on it. The ranger managed to get her off of the horse. Then he asked," Are you pregnant?" Next he said, "That is the only reason why something like that would happen." Furthermore, he explained "The scent of a pregnant woman drives the horse crazy." Consequently, that was the first and last time Wanda ever rode a horse.

Teen pregnancy is a bad idea. Wanda was 16 ½ years old and a junior in high school when she got pregnant and married. Her husband was an abusive spouse. After various attempts to complete high school, she was finally successful. Solomon didn't like it when he found out she was with child. So, he hit her very hard in her back. Nothing happened but Luke and John were okay with it.

Wanda suffered verbal abuse from people saying, "A baby having a baby." Her mother bought her beautiful clothes from Spiegel store to wear during her pregnancy. When Wanda delivered her son, her aunt was there to care for her and to make sure she rested. It was very difficult having children at a young age. Wanda wanted to party with friends but her mother told her "Take them with you." Soon, she begun to do things that she could do with her children, she went places where she was able to take them with her.

Wanda first husband was unfaithful, a drinker, and he gambled. Judas would go out drinking and return three days later starting fights so that she would stop complaining of his behavior. Women were calling and coming to her home looking for him. He would gamble away the house money. So, Wanda started hiding the money in an oatmeal box so she could survive from pay check to pay check. Every time she would leave the house, for any reason he would fight her when she returned.

Wanda was in a bad marriage, Wanda still wanted to complete her education. In 1970, she had two children from this marriage. She enrolled in Secretarial Training Program, she was paid a stipend to go there. She was doing very well but this program required perfect attendance. Wanda had a babysitter, however, one day when she went to drop her children off, the sitter just didn't answer the door. She missed class because she didn't have a sitter for that day. So, Wanda was asked to leave the program, she was so hurt. Wanda enjoyed the training and was almost finished when this happened.

In 1973, Halloween Day (10/31), Solomon gave Wanda a birthday party at his house. It was special because it was Wanda's first birthday party. They were both invited, but her spouse told her to go and that he would come later. He never came. After the party, Wanda went home to find the children's bunk beds, television, and other furniture missing. Her husband had gambled their furniture away to their neighbors in the court way building. At first, he lied about what happened. So, she asked a friend who witnessed the incident and she told Wanda the truth. She was very upset, the next day Wanda took her three children and left him. She didn't take anything else, she never returned. They've had plenty of fights but when he gambled their furniture away in a crap game, Wanda was finished with that relationship. She had had enough!

It was not easy to leave him because of her family beliefs. Her mother believed in one husband for life. However, Wanda couldn't see herself spending her life fighting and not having anything. Her mother meant well but she didn't have to live with him. Wanda's brothers wouldn't help get her clothes, or anything else because she had left him seven times before. Therefore, when she left without nothing they knew she was serious. As a result, they went for her things. They were married for 6 years. In 1974, Wanda divorced him for spousal abuse.

1974 – 1988
NEW OPPORTUNITIES
IN THE FACE OF
TRAGEDIES

CHAPTER 3

In 1974 -1978, Wanda was struggling financially, receiving welfare assistant and living in Section 8 housing. Her mother gave her $50 a month to help out. She was a single parent when she returned to school. Also, she worked summer jobs every year to buy her children school clothes. One place she tried to work was Daily Pay, she would wait all day for placement and didn't get placed. Next day, she would do the same routine for two weeks straight. It wasn't easy to get work in Babylon. One day they called her name and placed her in a factory to work. Wanda worked but she was so tire because she worked continuously for hours. At the end of the day, she was no longer focus. Wanda was working on a punch press machine and one worker was talking to her. She looked away to respond and someone snatched her hand out of the machine to prevent her from losing it. That was the first and the last day she worked there. However, Wanda worked other places like daycare centers, temporary jobs, clerical work, and college work study to make ends meet.

Pursuing opportunities are important but not easy to obtain when you have other responsibilities. Sometimes moving to another State might help brighten your future. When Wanda's children were young, she took them with her most places. Sometimes, John would watch them, or no one else would. She would start job training, or educational classes but was not able to finish because she didn't have a reliable babysitter. However, when her children turned 2 ½ years old, she would put them in the Head Start Program for a half day. Nevertheless, when she attended Two Year College she put Nehemiah, her youngest, in their daycare.

After Wanda's divorce, she prayed for a husband. In 1977, she met her second husband, she was trying to enter the apartment building where she was living. Wanda was dragging a cart of clothes behind her when the door swung open. She turned around and saw Timothy there holding the door so that she could get in. That was how they met. She lived on the third floor and he had a basement apartment in the same building. While Wanda attended night school at College, Timothy helped her by babysitting the children but he too was working. Finally, she got blessed after many years of unreliable sitters. Wanda got an excellent babysitter, she had a Title 20 home. She kept the children while Wanda attended day classes. She kept the same sitter until she finished College. Once the children were all in school it was a lot easier to work, or attend school at least part time.

Wanda enjoyed going to school. She graduated from Catholic High School and enrolled in Two Year College. When Wanda first went to college, she heard that Pell Grants would pay for the classes. She didn't know what classes to take. Wanda was so excited! She just wanted to learn more and more. Like a baby in a candy store, she wanted more! The second year, the school counselor called Wanda to her office and asked, "What is your major?" She answered, I don't have a major." At that point, the counselor suggested Liberal Arts major and she informed Wanda that she needed 19 additional credits to graduate. She asked, "What do you want to do?" She didn't want to leave college, but the counselor told Wanda that she may come back and take classes whenever she please.

So, Wanda took her advice, she needed nineteen credits to graduate that year. She wanted to finish them in one semester. Well, it wasn't easy with four young children. She had a good babysitter during the day but getting a sitter at night was a problem. So, Wanda registered for day classes 3 days a week and night classes 2 nights a week she dropped the children off to school and daycare, went to class herself. On the days that she didn't have class, she studied while the children were in school.

Her fiancé helped her by caring for the children at night. Wanda also studied at night after they were in bed. She was a slow reader so sometimes Wanda would be up all night and still took the children to school and went to class herself. Wanda also, cared for her ill mother by cleaning her house and she did the food shopping. Wanda made sure her mother's needs were met. One day after class she was waiting for the train on the platform at the Train Station. Wanda went to sleep while she was still standing and started to fall toward the train tracks. A stranger caught her before she fell. He said," Go home and get some sleep!" She was almost done with those classes, so she took his advice. Wanda graduated on 5/13/1978 from College with a 2 yr. Degree in Liberal Arts and she remarried that same year to her second husband.

After Wanda graduated from College, she worked at a Downtown Bank (1979). She worked full time as a Balancing clerk. It was not easy to find jobs in Babylon. She bought her attire from goodwill stores, she took the train downtown and walked all day putting in applications. She worked two months and three weeks at the Bank. She was forced to resign because she was very sick. Later, she took some college classes and clerical training (1980 -1982). Later, she transferred her completed college credits to another college to apply them toward a Bachelor degree, she used the clerical training to attain future employment.

It was the saddest time of her life and new opportunities were available to her. In 1983, a lot of things happened. Wanda moved to Promise Land, FL from Babylon, IL. She had never lived anywhere else but Babylon. But her husband, Timothy said there are jobs in the Promise Land. It is a land of Opportunity!!! Wanda left Babylon looking for career opportunities. She took a cab to the Airport. The cab driver was friendly. They talked for a while and then he suggested that she write a book about her life because some people never get out of poverty. He said it was important to share how she did it. Wanda never forgot his suggestion. When she arrived in the Promise Land, she got a part time job right away!

When Wanda was a child, her mother was very strict and sometimes abusive. However, she helped her move forward in life. She never gave up on her. Wanda loved her and still do. As an adult, once a month they shared apple pie and vanilla ice cream together. They went to High School and College together. When she was on public assistance, raising four children alone she loaned Wanda $50 every month to make ends meet until she didn't need it anymore. They spoke on the phone every day. Whether they disagreed about something or not. They were very close when her mother passed away. Wanda's mother loved her, wanted the BEST for her and nothing LESS! When her mother passed away 8/29/1983, she was only in the Promise Land for two weeks and two days. Wanda had to go back and take care of her mother's funeral arrangement. She was very sad but she did everything that needed to be done.

Mother's Day Card

M= Millions of good things she done for me.
O= Older: She had grown older.
T= Tear: The tears she cried for me.
H= Heart: She had a good heart.
E= Ear: She had a good listening ear.
R= Righteous: She was surely righteous.

When Wanda's mother died, she had only been in the Promise Land for two weeks and two days. The children reacted differently they were more playful and they acted out in school. They didn't verbally express any pain, but she knew how much they loved their grandma. Wanda couldn't afford to take them back to Babylon. So, they stay in Promise Land with Timothy. Wanda took an airplane flight back to Babylon to take care of the funeral arrangements, she cried most of the time. On the plane a man said," You must have lost your mother or someone close to you?" They talked for a while. He shared with her about a time he was in need and everything came together in a way that provided everything he needed. She didn't talk much, she just listened because she was so sad.

Not only did Wanda have to deal with her mother's death but her mother's insurance company didn't want to pay because she died before the two year requirement of her application. Wanda didn't have the money to give because of the big move to Promise Land. First, Wanda had to borrow plane fare to get back. Now, she needed money for her mother's funeral arrangements. She asked her father and he said, "No." She called a family meeting and everyone said that they didn't have it. Suddenly, one cousin, said, "I know your mother she helped a lot of people, she helped me too." She gave Wanda the money she needed.

Her brothers drove her wherever she needed to go but they asked her to take care of it. So, Wanda did, she cried through the whole ordeal and all the way back home. She learned a very important lesson from this, to preplan funeral arrangements. One way is to start a payment plan. Because when tragedy happened, it is always unexpected and very painful. So, at least you won't have to borrow money and cry at the same time.

Wanda returned home to the Promise Land, her family lived in an apartment. They rented a one bedroom apartment and had access to a pool. Wanda and her spouse took the bedroom, the five children slept on the hide-away couch. She had a new part time job with the school board. Timothy worked full time at a hotel. One day when the children were at the pool, Nehemiah spat on the deck and they were asked to move out. The family lived there about five or six months.

Next place they moved was to the Villas, it was a two story townhouse. They rented three bedrooms, it was enough room for the family. It was almost like their own little house. At this time, Wanda was working at a local bank (1984) as a full time Research Clerk. She used public transportation to get to work and it took her two hours each way. Sometimes, Timothy would drop her off and on the way they would experience car problems. As a result, she was late or had to miss work. Other times her mother-in-law would pick her up two or more hours after she'd finished her shift because she worked overtime on her job. One day while Wanda was waiting to be picked up from work, she was fired for being late. She was very sad but relieved at the same time, she did her best to get there on time. They needed reliable transportation they didn't have it. She worked there for eight months under these stressful conditions.

In 1984, Timothy and Wanda, both lost their jobs and the owner of their unit was required to pay a monthly maintenance fee of $50 to prevent homeowner association from foreclosing on his unit. He did not pay, again they were asked to move. Wanda's family were almost homeless, no income coming in, and the lease was up. They both looked for jobs. Wanda got a job at a local drug store as a cashier. They paid $3.55 an hour, she worked there for three weeks. She sought Emergency Assistance.

During this time, she was working for the government temporary for a year. It was first fourplex they lived in (1985), they lived above a man who was very aggravating. Every time they walked across the floor he hit the ceiling with a broom stick very hard. They were miserable, but tried to get along with him. Rumors was that he was a coke head and needed a lot of quiet after being up all night. One day they got into a conflict about this and they moved.

In 1985, the Canaan family moved to the first fourplex in Promise Land, FL. Timothy got a new job, and the family stayed there for five years. The first three years was okay but the last two years was very busy and dangerous. Wanda worked as a cashier at the grocery store for two months. Then, she worked as a part time teacher's assistant at the school board and she worked during the summer with the government. She moved from the first fourplex to another fourplex, it was a first floor and two bedroom unit that was located on the corner of the same block. One day while Wanda was hanging out clothes, there were gun shots, everyone ran into their houses until the shooting stopped. There were rumors that the reason for the gun shots was that a drug war was going on in the neighborhood. It didn't happen every day but it was always an unexpected event.

In 1987, Wanda father passed away, she only had her rent money. They were expecting a check but it was not there yet. She took the rent and returned to Babylon. When she got there a different aunt was upset and complaining because she had to pay for everything. Wanda explained her situation but she didn't want to hear it. She just walked away saying rude things about the family. The funeral home staff overheard everything and stated, she said that she used her rent to get here! Wanda paid her respects and returned home. When she got home the check had arrived, so she paid the rent.

They knew that they were in a poor environment, so they saved Timothy's checks for future housing and paid the rent with Wanda's income. They didn't plan to stay there very long but it was all that they could afford. At this time, she didn't have a permanent job but Wanda worked. First, she called different schools every school year and worked wherever there was an opening as a part time teacher assistant (1983-1984 & 1987-1988). Second, she worked with the government as a yearly temporary employee (1985-1986). Third, she worked at the grocery store for two months. Last, she worked during the summer with the government (1987).

Later, Wanda decided to seek a more permanent employment by pursuing a trade. So, she registered for Medical Assistant Training and completed all the course work for a Registered Medical Assistant on 8/19/188. After this, she was working at a Doctor's office (1988-1989). She finished her shift, but when she arrived home it was not safe to enter the apartment because of the gun shots being fired. She had to stay in her car on the floor with David and Timothy until the gun shots stopped. Surely, it was no longer safe to be in the second fourplex in the Promise Land. That summer 1989, she worked in a nursing home. At the beginning of school year, she worked with the school board (1989 -1991). She worked with a Cardiologist, for 11 months. It was a good job but she worked long and busy hours. As a result, she would miss class, she needed a less demanding job, so Wanda left there. Nevertheless, she was still attending college.

1989-PRESENT MILESTONES LEAD TO YOUR GOAL!

CHAPTER 4

Wanda's Christianity helped her to deal with failures, calamities, tragedies, and life as a whole. In 1989, her family was looking for a new home, they prayed and were standing on faith that they would find a better place to live. Her family found a new home in the Flyer, it was so beautiful! Then, they moved into their first three bedroom house and they were very happy!

Around this time (1990-1991) she was working part-time in the morning for the school board, and part-time in the afternoon at a preschool, while taking classes toward a University degree.

In 1992, Hurricane Andrew was calamity. Wanda and Timothy didn't go to a shelter but they prepared the best that they could. They had a small, battery operated radio to monitor the storm. When the storm came, it seem like it lasted forever. It was so noisy, a lot of rain, and very scary. They were in the hallway because there were no windows there. They heard something that sounded like a train whistle. Wanda went to the doorway of the hall while standing there, she looked into the family room, and saw a surge that looked like the ocean lifted up and came right at them! They lost 13 windows in their family room, their house was flooded, and water rose up to their knees. Wanda tried to put as much as she could in plastic bags to save their belongings. They never experienced anything like this before!

After the storm, it took a while for their house to be repaired. Their home was open to the public, they had no windows in the family room. They all slept in the living room to protect the house. One day someone tried to steal from them and the neighbors ran them off. During the day, the water and food truck came through the neighborhood, the

Insurance Agents came, too. At the park they gave hot meals to everyone regardless of financial status. Everything was destroyed, there were no stores opened to buy anything, It look like a war zone.

Later, they purchased a trailer home and put it next to their home. They lived there until their home was repaired. A lot of people moved away because they lost their homes. Wanda was working at the Head Start program. As a result, she was required to work under a tent and give to people in need of food. Some workers were relocated because of the storm.

Before their home was completely repaired, Wanda got very sick. She had a near death experience. She kept going to the doctor, they gave her medicine and send her home. This continued for three weeks, Wanda almost died. She couldn't go to the restroom either way, she couldn't eat or drink anything. She wasn't sleeping for three weeks and she couldn't stand more than two minutes. During a doctor's visit, she had a vision of Jesus on a Lighted path. She heard "Separation from Worldliness (II Corinthian 6:14-7:1). At this time, she was experiencing Hardship. Later, in 2011, she named one of her Sermon "Separation from Worldliness."

After that vision Wanda left the Promise Land and visited Joshua up North. She was not there for a night when he put her in the hospital (Hurricane Andrew Aftermath). When she was able to travel, Joshua brought her home. She was on six month leave from work. . Later, she got a full time position at the Head Start Program, she worked there until she started her internship at the University in 1993.

II Corinthians 6:14-7:1

14 Do not be yoked together with unbelievers. For what do righteousness and wickedness have in common? Or what fellowship can light have with darkness? 15 What harmony is there between Christ and Belial[a]? Or what does a believer have in common with an unbeliever? 16 What agreement is there between the temple of God and idols? For we are the temple of the living God. As God has said:

"I will live with them
and walk among them,
and I will be their God,
and they will be my people."[b]
17 Therefore,
"Come out from them
and be separate,
says the Lord.
Touch no unclean thing,
and I will receive you."[c]
18 And,
"I will be a Father to you,
and you will be my sons and daughters,
says the Lord Almighty."[d]
7:1 Therefore, since we have these promises, dear friends, let us purify ourselves from everything that contaminates body and spirit, perfecting holiness out of reverence for God. (Bible Gateway, 2011)

Idolatry is anything you put before the things of God. It can be a person, place, or thing. For example, being too busy to pray, to go to church, or to do your ministry. It can be a lifestyle that you are living contradictory to a godly lifestyle. However, it is important to put the things of God, first because they are most important.

Before, Wanda completed her University degree, she took classes to finish different trades. Joshua said, "You could be finished with your Bachelor degree by now! These are milestones." Wanda thought about it and decide to do whatever she needed to do to finish and to start her career of Teaching (Luke 1:37For no word from God will ever fail." (Bible Hub, 2011). It wasn't easy, one professor told her she wasn't college material because of a reading score on her entry exam. He advised her, to look up every word to build her vocabulary. Wanda did it and that improved her reading ability drastically. At the University, she met a woman while going to class. She said, "It will be like a Dark Tunnel with no end but keep taking the classes and you will see the light at the end of the tunnel." Wanda completed the course work and all required exams.

Wanda graduated from the University on 12/3/1993. She received a Bachelor Degree in Education. However, there were no teaching positions available. So, she prayed to God for a teaching position (I Peter 5:7Cast all your anxiety on him because he cares for you. (Bible Hub, 2011). In three days, she received three job interviews and was hired by the first school. She gave God all the glory, honor, and praise! When Wanda received her first check, she had a good feeling at the checkout counter knowing she didn't have to put anything back, or buy store brands to make ends meet.

On 5/7/1995, Wanda accepted Jesus as Lord and Savior over her life at Church as an adult. She accepted Jesus and was baptized as a child, but this time it was different. Because, now she was a responsible adult and would be held accountable for her decisions, this was serious! Wanda received a Certificate of New Birth from Church that day. At home, she provided shelter to troubled teens and young adults. Currently, most of them have jobs and their own homes. Some visit her on holidays and call her momma. She had a good relationship with their parents, too (1985-1995).

In 1998, Wanda had a dream of John's death. While, she was working full time, she completed her Master's Degree from the University on 10/31/1999. Also, she completed other job related certificates and licenses of her choice.

As a child she went to Catholic School and their church. However, in the evenings, Wanda and her mother visited other churches. In 1959, Wanda had a vision, she saw Jesus erasing her sins from the Book of life. Wanda was laying in her bed looking up (I Corinthians 12:4-11 Manifestation of Spiritual Gifts) (Fortune, 1987). This was her first vision, Wanda was attending Catholic School and their Church. In 1961, still in attendance at the same school, she was baptized at age 10, received confirmation, and her first communion. As an adult she still went to Catholic Churches and visited other churches.

In 1983, she left Babylon, IL and relocated to Promise Land, FL. Wanda joined a local church. She attended there until the year of 2000 but she never did any Christian service there.

Wanda was called, appointed, and anointed by God. After 9/11/2001, she went to the doctor and he said, "No work right now," So, she was on leave for about three months. During that leave (10/2001) first, she was very sick and she heard, "There is a church that needs you, Go and help her. You will sing Psalms." After that but the same month, Pastor came to visit her and she said, "I know I didn't visit when you were sick the first time but I am here, now." When, she felt a little better Wanda joined Christian Ministries. Second, on 11/2001, she was up preaching and teaching on Spiritual Gifts to the family using physical gifts and the Bible. She was spirit-led to preach and teach the Word of God. Joshua's friend, asked," Why didn't you use scripture references?" Third, one morning in the same month, while Wanda was watching a Pastor preach Romans 12:1-2 on television and she totally surrendered to the Holy Spirit for Christian Service (Romans 12:6-8 Motivational Gifts/Bible Teacher). She felt God's presence that day. Last, Wanda read the Bible in eight months, it was the first time she ever read the entire Bible.

In brief, in 1983 -1995, Wanda was a Home Missionary. She took in troubled teens to her home until they were able to return home, to prevent them from being homeless. In 1984, she studied Leadership at Church. In 2001, she was called by God to Christian church service. At the Christian Ministries, prayer was her first ministry, she always pray! Second, she was the Praise and Worship leader, she took private vocal lessons and piano lessons to upgrade her music skills. She visited the first church in 2002 and joined the choir for about one month. Third, Wanda taught Children church and Bible study to her grandchildren at home. Also, she was a substitute for the Sabbath School teachers for a long time.

Spiritual Gifts

Ministry Gifts/Five Fold Ministry (Ephesian 4:7-13)

1. Apostles (ambassadors) establish and strengthen churches.
2. Prophets (perceive) are inspired preachers, speak forth the message of God.
3. Teachers (communicate and research) instruct believers in the word of God.
4. Evangelist (church planter) called to preach the Gospel.
5. Pastors (preachers/teachers) feed and shepherds the believers.

Seven motivational gifts (Romans 12:6 -8)

1. Perceiver is the eye of the body of Christ.
2. Server is the hands of the body of Christ.
3. Teacher is the mind of the body of Christ.
4. Exhorter (encourager) is the mouth of the body of Christ.
5. Giver is the arms of the body of Christ.
6. Administrator (business) is the shoulders of the body of Christ. (I Corinthians 12:8 & Romans 12)
7. Compassionate person is the heart of the body of Christ.

Nine manifestation gifts (Corinthians 12:4-11)

1. Word of wisdom is the revelation of wisdom from God, what to do of what to say.
2. Word of knowledge is the revelation of information from God for a person, group, or situation.
3. Faith is wonder working faith, Move Mountains, and wait for results.
4. Gift of healing is divine healing through prayer or laying of hands.

5. Working of miracles is a demonstration of power and action of God.

6. Prophecy is an anointed proclamation of God to encourage, exhort, or comfort.

7. Discerning of spirits is to perceive what type of spirit is in the situation.

8. Various kinds of tongues is unlearned language given by the Holy Spirit.

9. Interpretation of tongues is the supernatural ability to express unlearned language spoken.

For examples: If a person has the ministry gift of an Apostle, the motivational gift of Helps (serving), and the manifestation gift of Miracles.

Another example: A person may have the ministry gift of Prophet, the motivational gift of Administration, and the manifestation gift of Healing. (Fortune, 1987)

Wanda previously had of dream of John's death. September to December 2001, she was on sick leave from work. He visited her in November 2001, he asked her to be his proxy over his end life, and that he didn't want to live on a machine. He was a dialysis patient.

She said that she would be his proxy but she didn't want to pull any plugs. Everything was normal, until June 2002 his first hospital stay. When he started having a lot of health issues, on July 13, 2002, he asked Wanda to pray the salvation prayer with him and she did. He accepted Jesus Christ as Lord and savior over his life that day. He was the first person that Wanda led to Jesus Christ. Also, she had just received the Holy Spirit and she surrendered for Christian service in November 2001.

Wanda returned to work in January 2002. After John was saved, whenever he went to the hospital Wanda would ministered to him. She visited weekdays after work and Saturdays after church. She sang praise and worship songs, read the bible to him, and watched the Christian station with him. Sometimes, they would share special meals and gifts.

He gave her a kitchen set for Christmas, a glass unicorn jewelry box, and a blue necklace for her birthday. She gave him a blue Good News bible for his birthday, and footprint cup, and flowers and they shared Kentucky Fried Chicken hot wings during their visits.

The last three weeks of John's life, after one of his dialysis visits, he was admitted into the hospital. The first week Wanda visited, he was restless and disquieted. Next day, she left church to visit him, in her car she read Isaiah chapters 40:1 -5; 53:1, and prayed before she visited him. He slept through the visit. The second week, he tried to recover by making an effort to get out of bed on his own. He wanted to go home but he was too sick at that time. She heard a voice on her way out of the hospital, saying "It's finished" (John 19:30 these were Jesus' last words on the cross before he died). Two days later, he looked and acted better. The last week and the first two days he called home. The third day, he had GI surgery because he wasn't eating properly. The fourth day, there was a problem after the surgery. The fifth day, he was in a coma but he responded when he heard our voices. On Saturday, 3/1/03, he died while Wanda was in Church while she was singing" I will worship thee/I will exalt thee." In 1998, The Lord Jesus told Wanda in a dream that her brother would die. He prepared her spiritually in 2001 for what was to come in 2003. He allowed her to share nine months of quality time with him. He gave Wanda a song to sing, scripture to comfort her and a word to guide her while she was going through this difficult time.

Isaiah 40:1-5; 53:1

Comfort, comfort my people,
says your God.
2 Speak tenderly to Jerusalem,
and proclaim to her
that her hard service has been completed,
that her sin has been paid for,
that she has received from the Lord's hand
double for all her sins.

3 A voice of one calling:
"In the wilderness prepare
the way for the Lord[a];
make straight in the desert
a highway for our God.[b]
4 Every valley shall be raised up,
every mountain and hill made low;
the rough ground shall become level,
the rugged places a plain.
5 And the glory of the Lord will be revealed,
and all people will see it together.
For the mouth of the Lord has spoken."
53:1 who has believed our message
and to whom has the arm of the Lord been revealed?
The good news about salvation, given by the prophets to Israel and the
nations, arm of the lord.
(Bible Gateway, 2011)

In sum of Wanda Christian service, she visited Luke, in 2002 and they
made a Praise and Worship Demo CD. On 3/4/2003 She wrote her
oldest brother's and her mother's obituaries. She was baptized as an adult
on 4/12/03 at Christian Ministries. On December 2003, during work
she was dismissing her students but it was a little quiet and she heard
"Leave Babylon" (Isaiah 30:21 whether you turn to the right or to the
left, your ears will hear a voice behind you, saying, "This is the way;
walk in it" (Bible Hub, 2011). To leave Babylon is Divine Deliverance
from captivity. Later, in 2009, Wanda wrote a Sermon series "Leave
Babylon."

In 2004, she preached a Trial Sermon on 2/9/04. She was ordained
as a Christian Minister for the first time online by Theological Seminary
on 3/3/04 and she wrote and coordinated a Christmas Program. In
2005 -2006, times when she felt okay, she created three holiday cards:
"What is a Traditional Thanksgiving?" "What is Family Support?"
And "Mother Day" (acrostic poem). However, she was very sick and

hospitalized two times. She prayed for her health in 2005 and she felt a burning sensation (Holy Spirit presence) her health was a little better but in 2006 Christian Ministries prayed for her healing. That was her last year of being hospitalized, Wanda haven't been in hospital for eight years. Praise God!!!

On 3/3/2007, she preached her first Sermon at Christian Ministries "Believe to Receive Your Healing" sermon, later she preached 13 more sermons. In 2008, She founded God is Greater Homeless Outreach Ministry, Incorporated. In 2009, she taught Children Salvation class and baptized six children (5 grandchildren and 1 friend). She received her Pastoral Ordination (4/11/2009) and Bible Teacher Certificate (7/4/2009) from Christian Ministries.

In 2010, she retired from the School Board. God is good! She worked for Public School Board for 21 years (Psalms 34:19but the Lord delivers him from them all; (Bible Hub, 2011). She started Full Time Associate Pastoral Ministry. She completed International School of Ministry/ Christian University 10/15/2010 and Pastoral classes Part I & II (5/28/2011).

Now, she have over 13 years' experience in ministerial service for the kingdom of Jesus Christ. Being an instrument that God can use. Also, she use her spiritual gifts to equip God's people to do his work and build up the church, the body of Jesus Christ. (Ministry Gifts/Five Fold Ministry (Ephesians 4:11-13) (Fortune, 1987).She have been a member of Christian Ministries from 10/2001 until now

Sermon Preached:

Believe to Receive Your Healing (3/3/2007)
How Do You Know When God Is Calling? (6/16/2007)
Know Your Adversary (7/28/2007)
How to Hear God's Voice? (9/1/2007)
New Covenant (10/19/2007)
Leave Babylon Series: God is Faithful! (9/19/2009)
Leave Babylon Series: The Fall of Israel (10/17/2009)

Leave Babylon Series: Living as Children of the Light (11/15/2009)
What is Our Covenant with the Lord? (12/19/2009)
Our Father (3/20/2010)
Power of the Tongue (4/3/2010)
Don't Forget God (10/2/2010)
Separation from Worldliness (3/19/2011)
How God Used Joseph's Spiritual Gifts to help others? (8/11/2012)

Prayers and Scriptures That Comforted Wanda During Her Struggles

John 10:10 Abundance of Life The thief comes only to steal and kill and destroy; I have come that they may have life, and have it to the full (Bible Hub, 2011)

Philippians 4:19 and my God will meet all your needs according to the riches of his glory in Christ Jesus. (Bible Hub, 2011)

Romans 8:28 and we know that in all things God works for the good of those who love him, who I have been called according to his purpose (Bible Hub, 2011)

THE LORD'S PRAYER

Matthew 6:9-13

9 "This, then, is how you should pray:
"'Our Father in heaven,
hallowed be your name,
10 your kingdom come,
your will be done,
on earth as it is in heaven.
11 Give us today our daily bread.
12 And forgive us our debts,
as we also have forgiven our debtors.
13 And lead us not into temptation, [a]
but deliver us from the evil one. [b]'

(Bible Gateway, 2011)

PSALMS 23

1The Lord is my shepherd, I lack nothing.
2 He makes me lie down in green pastures,
he leads me beside quiet waters,
3 he refreshes my soul.
He guides me along the right paths
for his name's sake.
4 Even though I walk
through the darkest valley, [a]
I will fear no evil,
for you are with me;
your rod and your staff,
they comfort me.
5 You prepare a table before me
in the presence of my enemies.
You anoint my head with oil;
my cup overflows.
6 Surely your goodness and love will follow me
all the days of my life,
and I will dwell in the house of the Lord
forever. (Bible Gateway, 2011)

INVITATION TO JESUS CHRIST

Do you know if you should die today that you will wake up in eternal life? If not, then choose today Life or Death. You may say "How will I do that?" It is simple. If you chose Death, it is to be eternally separated from Jesus Christ. But if you chose Life, then you will have eternal life with Jesus Christ.

This is what you must do today: Pray this prayer: Jesus, I accept you as Lord and savior over my life. Lord Jesus, I know I am a sinner and separated from you. But I believe you are the Son of God and that you died on the cross for my sins and rose again from the dead. So, that I may have eternal life. Jesus come into my life, forgive my sins, save me and take control of my life. I repent of my sins and now place my trust in you for my salvation. I accept the gift of eternal life. In Jesus name, Amen.

After this prayer, you will never be the same from this point forward!!! Scripture References:

John 3:16 For God so loved the world that He gave His only-begotten Son, that whoever believes in Him should not perish but have everlasting life.

John 14:6 Jesus said to him, I am the Way, the Truth, and the Life; no one comes to the Father but by me.

Roman10:9 because if you confess with your mouth the Lord Jesus, and believe in your heart that God has raised Him from the dead, you shall be saved.

II Corinthian 6:1 -13.

As God's co-workers we urge you not to receive God's grace in vain. 2 For he says, "In the time of my favor I heard you, and in the day of salvation I helped you."[a]I tell you, now is the time of God's favor, now is the day of salvation.

Paul's Hardships

3 We put no stumbling block in anyone's path, so that our ministry will not be discredited. 4 Rather, as servants of God we commend ourselves in every way: in great endurance; in troubles, hardships and distresses; 5 in beatings, imprisonments and riots; in hard work, sleepless nights and hunger; 6 in purity, understanding, patience and kindness; in the Holy Spirit and in sincere love; 7 in truthful speech and in the power of God; with weapons of righteousness in the right hand and in the left; 8 through glory and dishonor, bad report and good report; genuine, yet regarded as impostors; 9 known, yet regarded as unknown; dying, and yet we live on; beaten, and yet not killed; 10 sorrowful, yet

always rejoicing; poor, yet making many rich; having nothing, and yet possessing everything.11 We have spoken freely to you, Corinthians, and opened wide our hearts to you. 12 We are not withholding our affection from you, but you are withholding yours from us. 13 As a fair exchange—I speak as to my children—open wide your hearts also. (Bible Gateway, 2011)

CONCLUSION

Don't give up!!! Persevere to be successful. Take life one day at a time but planning is important. Stay focus on the GOAL!!!

Wanda overcame poverty through faith in God, by returning to school, preparing for a career while she worked menial jobs. Also, she worked during her children school hours. Everything that she has been through helped her to be the person that she is today. Wanda learned to survive and appreciate life. People can also learn from other people's mistakes. Most of all Wanda learned to pray and put her trust in God alone (Matthew 6:9 –13; Psalms 23; Philippians 4:19; Roman 8:28).

BIBLIOGRAPHY

Bible Gateway. (2011). Holy Bible, New International Version. Biblica, INC.

Bible Hub. (2011). Holy Bible, New International Version. Biblica, INC.

Fortune, D. &. (1987). Discover Your God-Given Gifts. Grand Rapids:
    Chosen Books.

ABOUT THE AUTHOR

Sheila Hodges is a University School graduate. She has a Master's Degree in Education and an Educational Specialist/Masters plus 36. Mrs. Hodges has nine job related licenses and certificates. She is a retired Elementary School teacher with twenty-one years of service. Also, she has an Associate Degree from an International School of Ministry and Christian University. Mrs. Hodges was ordained in 2003 as a non-denominational Charismatic assembly (Minister) and has been ministering for 13 years. Mrs. Hodges has served the Lord Jesus as a Pastor/Teacher and Founder of God is Greater Homeless Outreach Ministry Incorporation (2008). She has been married for 37 years. Also, she has five male children, 17 grandchildren, and 2 great-grandchildren. However, her life was not always this stable. It took plenty of faith in the one and only true God, (Jesus Christ), hard work, and determination to reach this point.

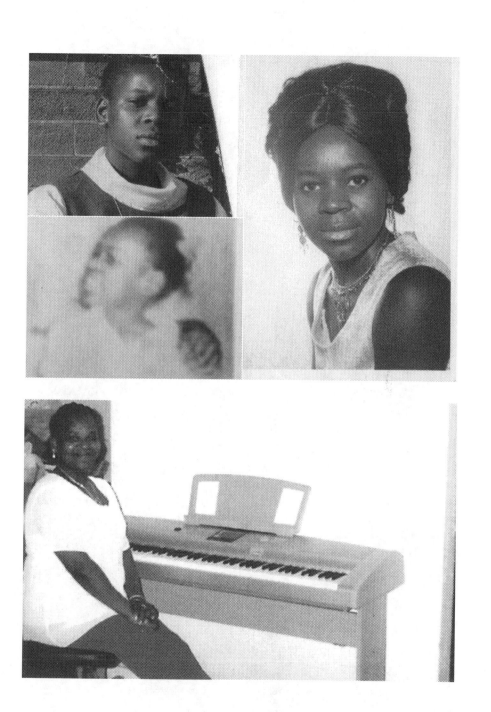